The Plague of the Tender-Hearted

poems by

Cindy Frenkel

Finishing Line Press
Georgetown, Kentucky

The Plague of the Tender-Hearted

*For Hannah Maud
and
In memory of Tom*

Copyright © 2020 by Cindy Frenkel
ISBN 978-1-64662-297-9 First Edition
All rights reserved under International and Pan-American Copyright Conventions. No part of this book may be reproduced in any manner whatsoever without written permission from the publisher, except in the case of brief quotations embodied in critical articles and reviews.

ACKNOWLEDGMENTS

My gratitude to the editors of the following publications, where these works have appeared, sometimes in different forms:

Insect Dreams miniature book series by Karen Anne Klein and Barrett Klein—"Ecdysis"
Mom Egg Review (MER)—"Surrender and Arrival"
Peacock Journal, e-zine—"The Anatomy of Color"
Peninsula Poets—"Slumber and Awakening" (First Place, Family Category, Michigan Poetry Society) and "Plate Tectonics" (Third Place, Margo LaGatutta Memorial Award, Michigan Poetry Society)
Pink Panther Magazine—"The Last to Leave," "And still," and "Arrival"
Poetica—"Who'd Notice?" (as "Grammatical Choices")
PRISM (Lawrence Technological University)—"Through the Criss-Cross Thicket," "Elegy," "Devout Atheist," and "An Outing of Boating"
Renaissance City Magazine for the Arts, e-zine—"Things I Have to Forget to Fall Asleep," "How You Said Goodbye," "And still" and "Facts" (as "Imagine It")
The Alembic—"Our Winter Pool" originally as "Winter Pool"
The MacGuffin—"In the Classroom," "Keeping Quiet," "Three Generations," "Things I Have to Forget to Fall Asleep," "Lending the Book" (as "Miracles"), and "Goodbye"

Publisher: Leah Maines
Editor: Christen Kincaid
Cover Art: Marvin Frenkel, portrait of his daughter, Cindy, as a child
Author Photo: Olga M. Klekner
Cover Design: Elizabeth Maines McCleavy

Order online: www.finishinglinepress.com
also available on amazon.com

Author inquiries and mail orders:
Finishing Line Press
P.O. Box 1626
Georgetown, Kentucky 40324
U. S. A.

Table of Contents

Things I Have to Forget to Fall Asleep 1

In the Classroom 2

Keeping Quiet 3

Slumber and Awakening 4

Arrival 5

Surrender and Arrival 6

Raising her is better than 7

Our Winter Pool 8

Lending the Book 9

Facts 10

How You Said Goodbye 11

Who'd Notice? 12

Elegy 13

I am sick of poems 14

Three Generations 15

The Last to Leave 16

Through the Criss-Cross Thicket 17

The Anatomy of Color 18

An Outing of Boating or Let's Jump Overboard 20

Plate Tectonics 21

F on the Quiz 22

And still 23

This has been 24

Dusk Love 25

My Father Insists on Eating Meat Again 27

Bad Neighborhood 28

Devout Atheist 32

Ecdysis 33

Things I Have to Forget to Fall Asleep

Just before evening's end, the list begins:
three piles of laundry, like the mind, divided,
the electric bill, that intrepid old *LIFE*
magazine I've been meaning to…
Churchill on the cover
reminds me of Clementine.
The sad oranges and arugula that need
to be tossed. In New Orleans,
tumbling churches, streets under water.
Another Malaysian airplane missing.
My three cousins
all horribly ill at once,
an outbreak of honesty.
Wondering when our time will be up:
first my mother, then my brother,
slow sinking, rapid fire.
First love, husband, marriage implodes.
A love never to be found again,
still it aches like a mad desire,
the match that can't catch fire.

In the Classroom

I mention my brother died by suicide.
The room stops.

In ten years of teaching, I tell them,
I have never said this before.

Yet they lost one student this past fall
so the dean invites me to share

what I wish I couldn't readily recall.
Bringing forth this brother now, and hours later, too,

to another class, on this same industrial carpet,
where long Formica tables stand in rows,

as if order meant reason,
the segue's natural as a river's artery.

There is no rustling of paper. Even the leaves
stop bobbing out the window; the fog lifted seconds ago.

The frames are a still life.
In backpack pockets, cell phones emit waves insensate.

I've introduced them to Septimus Smith and Virginia Woolf herself
and Anja Spiegelman, whose photo they have seen only once

but mostly know only as a mouse. Mental illness
is just that, an illness, and addiction is just that.

For years I took such illness as a personal affront
—depression, addiction—inexorably joined.

Rocks in her pockets. Walk in the water.
Let me know, I say. Ask, I tell them, when someone's depressed—

ask the question, be specific: *Are you suicidal?* Remember,
Not Really is a *Maybe*. Anything other than a *No* is a *Maybe*

and a *Maybe* is a *Yes*. A *Maybe* is always a *Yes*.

Keeping Quiet

Father, when you tell my child, *No, speak softly, ladies don't yell,*
I relive your punishment. I was four years old.
How loud a small body can scream!
To suppress it, impossible.
Before watching TV in the den,
or whatever it was you did,
you locked me in the garage.
I couldn't come in, until
I acted *like a human being.*

Night dark, cement walls cold,
expecting someone to break in, take me,
I pounded on the garage's thick door, yelling
until exhaustion overcame
my body, vocal cords frayed.
Even then, ignored.
Sliding into your Cadillac's back seat,
Mother's station wagon beside,
I breathed in its awful leather newness,
stared at tufted buttons, tried resting without sleep.

Now, I get my daughter out of your home,
I let her scream.
Her beautiful, tiny, perfect self.
I let her scream.

Slumber and Awakening

Blue eyes searching, lips latching on,
she wouldn't let go of me until sleep took hold.
Now, nearly grown and hazel-eyed, she studies Latin
in the other room, eats pasta that she's rolled.
She alternates between two beds, two homes,
with the constancy of female friends.

Waving her hands as if conducting the wind,
she talks of boys, first-shaven. Invisible, I drive.
Girls in the back seat, their voices still high and sweetly soft,
overlay each other's phrases in counterpoint.
There must be a goddess I've never read about
who gathers stars only to disperse them.
She opens her palms and stars spill out,
enough to occupy the universe.
The road ahead's so bright it almost hurts.

Arrival

You are watercolor in the distance,
a fleck of green against gray,
a Chinese landscape.

You stand in the gazebo.
The gazebo's poles are brushstrokes;
you are blurry in fog.

Morning arrives. A willow interrupts
the red disk. Your brown boots
disturb the dewy grass.

Surrender and Arrival

Liquid gushing down my thighs
wakes me instantly, 5 a.m.,
trails my path, bed to bath;
phone calls to Dr. Markowitz,
my mother, the sudden tears.

At the hospital,
Completely transverse,
Markowitz says, rubbing my shoulder,
Emergency cesarean, promises
I'll be fine, has me sign
that my death wouldn't be their fault.
My last moment on earth, in a room
with linoleum tile, fluorescent lights buzzing.
Wheeled to the O.R., teeth chattering,
Markowitz with me all the way, hand in mine;
strangers move mechanically
around my nakedness.

Let me know when you begin, I tell Markowitz.
I've already cut into you, he says,
then asks if I want to watch.
Watch? *Yes* I want to, *Yes,*
and the mirror rises like a revelation:
My blood splatters—he lifts the seven red layers
of my belly, slips his hands under my skin
as if reaching into the slit of an envelope.

Tiny birth-wax buttocks, shimmery,
and he turns the small body over.
A daughter! Her first breath!
I'm looking at myself from above,
as they say one does in death.

Raising her is better than

parrot tulips newly drooping in an Aalto vase,
French gardens, English clotted cream,
playing footsie, Botticelli's women at the Uffizi.
Swiss chocolate in Switzerland, Russia's golden domes,
tunnels of the Vatican, lazy days at home.
Endorphin release from exercise,
China's Great Wall, dinner in Bologna.
It's superior to them all.
Hummingbirds up close. Cyrano.
Cold water on a sweltering day. Mozart's concertos.
Taking off stilettos. The scent of lilacs
wafting through the window. Summer's warm breeze.
The relief of a long-awaited sneeze.
A good night's rest, Motown, rainforests, newborn pets.
The Holy Wall in Jerusalem.
Our sweatiest, most loving sex.
Meeting with Gandhi in a private reception.
Long, slow kisses that led to her conception.

Our Winter Pool

I remember my father and me
running out his studio door in bathing suits,
steam rising. He went first, and then
we both went under. A few minutes treading water,
and then we lay, heads pillowed,
side by side on covered mats.
We talked quietly, breath haloed
beneath a canopy of trees—pines'
white boughs bowing in moonlight,
sugar maples dredged in snow—
curved lines frosting
the blue-white night softly coated,
stars dotting sky.
We dipped our heads under
so our hair wouldn't bead with ice.
We spoke now and then, mostly watched.
I ran and he followed, back into the studio;
we slipped on terrycloth robes.
Upstairs, when I fell asleep
my day slipped easily away,
and night was everything I wanted.

Lending the Book
in memory of Hymie Groskind

When I dropped by your house to lend your wife a book,
the second night of Chanukah, you asked my daughter
to light the menorah. Only three, she held the candle lit
—for anyone else I'd have protested—
but there you were in your short sleeves: 7 7 3 2 3.
I'd never seen your numbers before.
They cattled you well, each European 7 evenly crossed.
When you returned to Auschwitz with your son,
they charged admission; you shook your head,
held out your arm, and they let you in.
Survivors always travel for a birth or a wedding—
your son's wedding, with your two old friends
from New Jersey and Philly, the three of you,
together, again, in three consecutive numbers.

Facts

Near war's end, he began
the impossible death march
from the outskirts of Auschwitz,
one emaciated man carrying his emaciated friend
for nine days, the sheer God luck
of not being shot.

How You Said Goodbye

Tom, I couldn't get into
the skin you so desperately
wanted to crawl out of
      even though we began in the same womb
not two years apart.

I didn't foresee
what now appears so transparent—
those last months
     your hints
and apologies.

I yearn to go back
to the illusion that
our family's intact,
to have your wide wrist wear this
big Cartier watch,

for you to be dressed
in these sweaters now stacked
in cedar against the moths.
  Simply to hear your voice again
on the phone, your tone rising, past
effusive, brimming with affection:

                     ter!
Sweet   *Sis-*

     Sis-

Sweet
                  teeeer!

     (Being present with emotion
     was a punitive condition.)

There you were repeating, with tender candor,

I love you, Cin.   *I love you, Cin.*   *I love you, Cin.*

I didn't recognize goodbye.

Who'd Notice?
>*in memory of my brother Tom*

At first, my mother preferred to say *took his life.*
I said: *Suicide.*
People thought he overdosed, which made sense.
The exit wound was so high up
an oversized yarmulke covered it, and my family reversed
his casket's direction. (Who'd notice?)
Open casket—
Smartest thing we did, my dying mother said.

No one walked around the backside
where full-blown roses were displayed.

I glanced at him: high cheekbones, sculpted face,
angelic in his white robe, one diamond stud.
I returned to the back room, preparing to perform.

Naturally, my parents rushed home,
brothers, cousins.
An estranged cousin
perused the fine Federal furniture.

The whole city was in the dining room. On the wall
my grandmother's miniatures, verre églomisé silhouettes.
Note the title of the prettiest, *The Happy Family.*
Yes, I know Tolstoy was right, we are not all alike.

One woman asked,
How did he do it? Was he alone?
A man said, *You have his dog?*
Yes, I promised, if anything…
So you had a warning, he said. (Who'd notice?)

I woke up, thought Tom wasn't really gone,
descended the steps to my dining room,
saw each shiny black letter engraved,

The family of on cream paper.
No one minded I picked out a casket
too ornate. (Who noticed?)
Later, I sent myself away,
repeated, *He put a bullet in his head.*

Elegy

O lost brother in your grave,
I leave my assemblage:
two twigs, a stone. I am alone
above grass over bone.

I am sick of poems

about suicide and artists whose work
is earmarked with it, as if their exits
were major accomplishments.
Why did it ever draw me in?
Parker's clever, rejected options.
Arbus, Rothko, Berryman.
Plath should have baked only bread in the oven;
Sexton's garage door could've unhinged.
Oh, let's not go on with the whole list—

Tom, you put yourself in daunting company.
But that crisp November morning of your funeral,
I walked your nearly feral dog; his nostrils read the breeze.
Collage of wet leaves, rust, gold, green,
littered damp pavement, glistening memento mori.

Three Generations
in memory of BPF

Roles reversed, everything askew:
My daughter's nine, my mother's seventy-two,
and now they are the exact same weight.
My daughter walks with my mother's gait.

My mother, robed, looks up from her wheelchair
as I brush what's left of her gray hair,
and watch my daughter spoon-feed her ice cream.
Strands of hair are coming down like rain.

They used to sit cross-legged on the floor,
playing "bakery" with candles shaped like tortes,
made brownies for their picnics on the sand—
I watched them in their swimsuits, hand in hand.

Where are you off to? Her first solo drive.
She looks away. *To visit Grammy's grave.*

The Last to Leave

While disappearing from her body,
my mother stayed in her condo,
her fragile presence evaporating;
skin outlining bone after bone,
heart's small pulsing
through what was left of her breast,
up-down, up-down breath.

My mother was departing
from the feet up—
mornings, we'd peel the sheet,
the hospice nurse and I,
from her cold, blue-mottled legs.
Hearing, the last to leave—

Tom is on the other side,
I whispered, bending over,
stroking her hair, those brief,
longest days of my monologues—
and her parents were there,
her sister, her cousin Bob,
his sister with the dour expression,
whose name I forgot, she knew,

and I knew it was lights out
in the big, beautiful city
I once lived in, my winding street her veins.
She finally went completely still
and then I slid open the balcony door
so her soul could fly away.

Through the Criss-Cross Thicket

I.

Amid the thrum of rain, I lie
sprawled on worn, cotton sheets
side by side with my tuxedo cat; her eyes startle—
one jade green, one sea-blue, of equal hue,
my face reflected in her irises, the black diamonds,
and her pink pads stretch towards me,
that black tail rising, tipped with a white dot, her exclamation point.
She nestles in, whirring, and there my dreams begin…

II.

Lost as once in Hastings, East Sussex,
returning solo to my friend's
through the criss-cross thicket late in day,
brushing against brush, spines of thorny branches,
my bearings gone, long shadows,
animal sounds, my heart's thumping
as arms of branches turn ominous
in their clarity. Suddenly, God's reprieve—
a clearing—this open field, its ferny lushness.
Here, clear, sky bright, one blue shade,
wide-water view, panorama of stone buildings dotting
around that old Castle, everything spread out like a great quilt.

III.

In my old, uneven house,
ordinary loveliness everywhere,
aging oak floor, grains swirling
into darker grains, as when I stir batter,
watch it eddy into itself,
lines in my palms, patterns of a fingerprint—
and music—yes—Bach's flute concerto
in the background, notes gliding, merging
these worlds: cat, white sheets, wood floor,
rain's soothing static, its wavy lines
trickling down windowpanes.

The Anatomy of Color

I.

Green yields itself to us
this time of year,
the hopeless birch, felicitous willow,
and even the pink tulips,
with their green stands and leaves,
bend over as most any flower would
in such a breeze. Air rushes in
with the smell of green, tries to articulate
the pure cerulean of the sky
and fails. But somehow the sweet
smell lingers, and the willow
mops the sky. Through the miniature gray boxes
of the screen door I see: two red metal
chairs with their fanned backs,
a yellowish straw mat to wipe one's feet on,
and the lawn's vast expanse,
a variety of greens—mint, army, pine.

The paper with its black-on-white
characters is tossed near the door;
its scroll shape rolls, morning
after morning, just beyond the green.
Incarnadine, slender fingers push open the door.
Coffee's smell wafts
through this small house,
and look: The table's ready, the white
porcelain cup reflecting the silver
of a fork, *sizzle* then *splatter*
of breakfast cooking.
Doesn't the sky seem bluer today?
The colors outside more
of what they are, each piece of fruit,
every dirty lawn chair, each blade of hair.

Even the air carries the smell of color:
apple blossoms' explosion, pink and white.
Brushing a mosquito away from the face,
feeling that calm
at seeing lawn, gray-brown bark

of a tree, violet in a bud, *green*,
green as only summer, in a stem.

II.

Up the brown steps,
a plaid dress on the chair is waiting
to be worn, and loafers are abandoned
in the corner, brown leather
staring at brown leather. A few amber hairs
in the brush, amber which will grow darker,
then lighter, gray, gray-white, softer.

Night is the darkest blue punctuated
by white dots. Iridescent blue wings flutter
between brown trees, and individual nouns
are trying to spell *Forever*.
Color and form divide, distinguish,
modify, as everything ages.
The moon is only a chip of gold, a transmutation
of its old substance, adequate light
to catch the lilacs bobbing. The elm
in the back of the house has been standing
for hundreds of years, the blue wings
flickering for maybe a moment.

An Outing of Boating or Let's Jump Overboard

Never mind that the view is exquisite.
This is not what I call a pleasant visit.
We are someplace remote, afloat
on Lake St. Clair in my in-laws' boat.

I thought that all was atypically calm,
but they're ready again to start a storm.
She confides disappointment (she's usually the one)
from months ago at something we'd done.

The wind blows; the sail ripples *rat-a-tat-tat*.
Eating, swaying—that's how we sat.
Two of them and two of us.
Do we have to stay? We must.

There is no place to go: We're completely trapped.
And then the wind steals my expensive hat.

Plate Tectonics

Plates shift, cause and effect—
friction wears against the final straw.
One grinds over the other; less is left.

Marriage dissolves and you reflect
what you sensed (unseen, there really was more).
Plates shift, cause and effect.

No widow's wardrobe yet utterly bereft,
sudden weight loss, you're numb to the core.
One grinds out from under the other; less is left.

You've a daughter to protect.
Gingerly walk: There is no floor!
Plates shift, cause and effect.

For a while you receive a monthly check,
pay the bills, cross out each chore.
One grinds over another. Less is left.

And now you start to live beyond the wreck,
home orderly and safer than before;
plates shifted, cause begat effect.
One ground over the other; less is left.

F on the Quiz

Q: Why didn't Cinderella's glass slipper disappear at midnight?
A: I never had a clue, which bothers me still.

Q: Who said: *Money doesn't care who owns it?*
A: My brother told it to me, but he's no longer here to ask.

Q: Who wrote the following?
Daffodils are old-fashioned telephones.
A: Actually, May Swenson used phones as their parallel—it took over forty years to figure *that* one out.

Q: To whom do you attribute this quote?
Divorce is amputation by tearing.
A: My friend Jan. She was correct.

And still

When you step out
of your own door
every morning the crisp air stings
with kisses, laughter erupts like a wild stream—
you never dreamt you would find
your deepest love alone.

This has been

my biggest surprise.
Large, tattooed man,
shaved head, hoop in ear,
love in air, old-
fashioned protector.
Factory worker, defender.
He invites me for hors d'oeuvres.
Camille Saint-Saëns, Jay Ungar, Annie Lennox,
he likes them equally,
as well as felling trees.
He shoots straight, eats his quarry,
donates what he can't.
He presents me with a rolled
khaki-colored sheet; the only paper
from his home long enough to protect the gift
he's grown. Unfurling reveals a human
target, complete with scoring rings,
cradling one red, massive, long-stemmed rose.

Dusk Love

Sky darkens, night settles in,
and I crave your soft skin,
yeoman's muscles,
warmth of arms, biceps' light hair,
the rise and fall of your chest,
its keloid scar-stripe down the center.

This, Love, is the plague of the tender-
hearted, the very limits of it all—
I remember the surgeon
saying men like you would be tender longer,
barrel-chested, big guys.
After they moved you
from intensive care
you began to relax,
until your heart raced,
the alarm sounded,
a machine bleating
Do Not Resuscitate
repeating its death knell;
the staff swarmed
around you, and you
spoke of your father's death.
They shooed me away.
You wanted water.

Walking with the nurse
to the kitchen, opening the freezer,
I held my head in, fanned my watery eyes,
filled your cup, returned with arms outstretched.
The staff busy around you still,
speaking in their foreign language.
Later, when it was calm again, you moved
into silence.
I tried to read, but looked up,
kept looking up,
at your beautiful, flushed face,
high cheekbones,
small, straight nose,
ombré gray goatee,
wild Russian eyebrows,

wires all in the right order,
the whole of you, the absolute whole.

My Father Insists on Meat Again

His oven is broken, sparse cupboard, no spices;
I slice the meat thin, pour grapeseed oil,
onion soup mix, toss pepper in.
Sautéing mushrooms, sizzling oil, I watch them shrink
and my father is shrinking too,
forgets conversing with my daughter an hour ago.

He's in the bed where my mother died, sleeping away the day.
Shades drawn, ratty fabric's dotted with holes,
starlight slipping through. The ocean's on the other side,
dusk seeps into scalloped empty spaces
by the curtain rods, fabric's fallen from its hooks.

He has swum a half hour—busy day!—today.
When his girlfriend isn't visiting, he wants to curl up with his aide.
We tell ourselves *This isn't him.*

I smash new potatoes—red, white,
dress radicchio, romaine. *Toss! Toss!*
For the fifth time, I insist he rise from bed—
and here he appears: my father!

My father, in his blue bathrobe.
This is the man who tutored me in math,
who bent the fish spine at the dinner table
marveling at its elegance. Here is the man
who wore his beret in the Jeu de Paume,
sketching in his little pad his impression
of the Impressionists as onlookers looked on.

The table's set. I present his plate.
He reads my menu's curly script, then laughs:
Frenkel's Impromptu Boeuf avec Chanterelles.
We bite in—tender meat dissolves
on tongues, potatoes smooth and warm. *Delicious!* he says.

Prone to quoting *Iolanthe* these days, he begins:
"I wouldn't say a word that could be reckoned as injurious.
But to find a mother younger than her son is very curious."

We smile. He nods.

Bad Neighborhood

I.

Stars sprinkle like salt.
Your dog goes in and out.

II.

Thrice-trashed,
I kept going back,

wanting to make that childhood right.
My second mother, Tina, on the bright

green grassy lawn, teary with dew.
If I could freeze the picture, I wouldn't feel such pain—

and I'd hear your voice joking—
with a nickname for everyone.

III.

It took me 18 years to publish:
Shame was an accessory to your death,

as was your gun. Your exit wound
was the final way you left—

the needle did its number
but we performed the larger theft.

IV.

Parts of Michigan are vast, desolate—
farmland for miles, silos near carpets of grain,
and cows, their black spots
whole countries on a map.

IV.V.

Father's business went under years before.
Look good, look good—

Take out the trash. Let in the cat.
May I have directions please?

X.

After my mother's cancer,
sickness pummeled in;

we couldn't see before us,
blood-garnet blurred the way—

traffic lights dangled like earrings,
emeralds fulgent in rain.

Trees bending as if pleading.
Lights directing: *Come, Go,*

and love was a cat
arching against a leg, leaning into loss.

VI.

I inherited a showy necklace,
gowns of beaded silk—
all I'd wanted
was to be held when I was five pounds,
drink my mother's milk.
(Five pounds, so small!
Don't touch—she's fragile in glass.)

VII.

Our mother had six months to live they said. You, thirteen years clean—
you blamed our mother's cancer for your relapse.

Chemo in her veins, heroin in yours.
We couldn't see your disease, dire as hers—

findings might confirm our failings, so ignore.
We gathered round the matron, elegant,

awed by her grace—
yet I pleaded for help for you,

and my voice again dismissed—
the only girl, the poet! (What a waste!)

I said how sick you were—
Shut Up! they shook their heads at me.

VIII.

I cannot…it.

IX.

Our father thought
you were sleeping upright
on the couch—
went closer,
rigor mortis had set in—

IX.V.

I screamed. Pay phone, gas station,
in a different state
and in a different state,
grateful to have called the cops
to meet them at your door—

VIII.

Petrichor, and the fern sprouts;
spiny, spindled shadows

of sage leaves, overflow,
waterfall of tiny, chartreuse lines.

In morning's light, one stem's shadow flits
onto my open palm, dappled sun rains down.

IX.

I do not wear my wedding ring;
I wear my mother's wedding ring.
My father's withering.

I wear his wedding ring.
(I show him this.)
He doesn't know what day it is.

VIII.V.

Mary Shelley read at her mother's grave,
made rubbings with the letters,
as if naming is saying and saying is sense.

Galway wrote of the Shelleys,
the lie, the myth, and love
is never free—

and a prayer is only a thought.
I want to send up those loving prayers
and declare *yes* today

because I was anchored in the living dying,
seven years I was anchored in the sinking.
Living is always dying.

Now I follow a winding path,
I, the one who could never read a map.

X.

Your couch was soaked.
A gun went off.

Devout Atheist

Faith is invisible, I say.

He replies, *No empirical data!*
Absurd! Like saying the sky's red.

Sometimes it is, I say.

Ecdysis

In Indonesia, photographs are shot
of the bright green grasshopper
molting from her ghostly shell,
dangling from a hairy stem.
Emerging from her milky replica
(that sheer, articulated exoskeleton,
luminescent in the sun), she hangs
together with her former sheath, upside down
and side-by-side, until her newest self is dried.

Additional Acknowledgments

Two stellar poets have been invaluable, serving as kind, wise, and encouraging anchors: Molly Peacock and Mary Jo Firth Gillett. Molly also ushered in my beloved muses, Julia Shipley and Carla Drysdale. (Alice Quinn, I'm so glad you connected me with Molly years ago.) Much gratitude and love to Marcia and Larry Ferstenfeld. A wide net of people helped keep me afloat—Roeper friends, New York literary ones, childhood and high school ones, as well as the Detroit poetry community and Sunday morning circle—I cannot express my appreciation enough. Thanks also to Nancy Adams, Carol Was, Barbara Larew Adams, Dorit Silver, Julie Cummings, Nick Samaras, Olga Klekner, Karen Klein, Sue Shapiro, Paula Allen, Jan Krist, Don Major, Kathleen Olsen, Adiva Sotsky, Wynn Cooper, Ela Harrison, and Jim Zeman. I'm honored to have worked with the good people at InsideOut Literary Arts Project spreading our passion for poetry. Special gratitude to our workshop group. Jan Mordenski's close reading of my work always helped. Alice Phillips, your imprint is everywhere. Tina Brooks, Nancy Sestok, Galway Kinnell, "Mrs. Walden," Phyllis Winshall, Bonnie Sherr, and Maria Costantini are no longer alive, but their influence has forever changed me. Thanks to Christen Kincaid for her careful editing, and the team at Finishing Line Press, especially Leah Maines, who said yes. Chris Rhein quoted Mary Jo saying "The plague of the tender-hearted." Mary Jo let me steal it, even though she doesn't remember saying it. Thank you to my family, especially Nelson Lande. Gratitude to M.G.H., a big tattooed man, the most eccentric, patient man I know. Hannah, you are the reason.

Cindy Frenkel's essay "15 Lessons from 9 Years of Teaching" appeared in *Writers in Education*. Her essay "My Brother & Kate Spade" was in *The Jewish News* and her remembrance "Galway Kinnell and the Blue Button-Down," was in *The Southampton Review*. She served as a Writer-in-Residence with InsideOut Literary Arts Project (iO), which brings working poets into Detroit public schools; her essay about that is in the anthology *To Light a Fire*. Her poetry has been in numerous journals, and her prose has appeared in publications ranging from *Vanity Fair* to *The New York Observer*, where she was a columnist. She co-authored *100 Essential Books for Jewish Readers* with Rabbi Daniel B. Syme and was the writer/editor of the Detroit Institute of Arts magazine (DIA). She teaches literature and creative writing for video gamers at Lawrence Technological University. She has an M.F.A. from Columbia University and was a Hambidge fellow in 2018. For more information, please visit *www.cindyfrenkel.com.*

www.ingramcontent.com/pod-product-compliance
Lightning Source LLC
LaVergne TN
LVHW041604070426
835507LV00011B/1309